Original title:
The Infinite Search for Life's Answer

Copyright © 2025 Creative Arts Management OÜ
All rights reserved.

Author: Ryan Sterling
ISBN HARDBACK: 978-1-80566-206-8
ISBN PAPERBACK: 978-1-80566-501-4

Questions in the Cosmos

Why is the sky blue and wide?
Is it just the ocean's eyes?
Do stars twinkle, or are they shy?
Awaiting secrets, no surprise.

What if cows really jumped the moon?
Or socks felt lonely, worn in pairs?
Do aliens play a cosmic tune?
While we ponder life in chairs.

Threads of Curiosity Weaving Truth

If cat videos are a path to bliss,
Do dogs scroll too, with secret paws?
When will we find that answer's kiss?
Or is it hiding in our flaws?

Do plants whisper when we walk by?
Or are they just rooted in their place?
If nature talks, would we reply?
Or stare blankly, lost in space?

Shadows of Wisdom in Twilight

Why is it that we laugh and snore?
Does the night breeze have tales to tell?
Will we unlock the universe's door?
Or just enjoy a comfy shell?

Is wisdom a light bulb that flickers bright?
Or just a shadow playing tricks?
Like a magician in the dark night,
Hiding answers up his sleeve, thick.

The Journey of Unseen Roads

If life's a road with twists and turns,
Do GPS systems know the plot?
Are we the stars that brightly burn?
Or just lost travelers in a dot?

Can laughter guide us through the haze?
Or is it just a silly game?
As we seek meaning in odd ways,
We might just end up with the same.

Echoes from the Depths of Silence

In the depths of thought I roam,
Chasing echoes, far from home.
The answers giggle, hide, and play,
While I just fumble, day by day.

Questions dance like butterflies,
In my mind, they wear disguise.
I trip on riddles, oh so sly,
Why do I even try?

Between the Lines of Existence

Between the lines, I write and scribble,
Hoping for clarity, just a nibble.
But words turn wobbly, like jelly beans,
And wisdom feels like cotton candy dreams.

I ask a tree, it shrugs and yawns,
A squirrel chuckles at my dawns.
What's the point of searching so?
When all I get is squirrel show?

Paths Woven with Questions

I wander paths, all twist and bend,
Hoping to find a clever friend.
But every tree has jokes to tell,
In riddles, I just slip and fell.

A sign points left, a sign points right,
I'm caught in this curious plight.
Where's the road to truth, I plea?
Did I just miss it with my tea?

In the Garden of Longing Hearts

In a garden lush with hopes and dreams,
Heartflowers bloom, bursting at the seams.
But bees buzz laughter as they sip,
While I just wonder, am I equipped?

Every blossom has a query bright,
Like "Why do socks just lose their fight?"
I pluck a petal, feeling bold,
Only to find silence, uncontrolled.

Shadows of Existence

In the alley of worries, I once lost my shoe,
A sock puppet laughed, and who knew it too?
I asked the fridge, its hum was so wise,
It stared back with silence, a food-filled disguise.

The cat on the window, she naps in the sun,
I ponder my purpose; she's just having fun.
The goldfish keeps swimming, it's lost in the stream,
While I chase my thoughts like a half-baked dream.

Fleeting Footprints in Time

A squirrel asked me about yesterday's news,
I said, 'I've misplaced it, but any excuse!'
It twitched its small nose, then ran up a tree,
While I stood with my coffee, just wishing for glee.

Was that a deep thought or just lunch on my mind?
I swear the old bench tried to help, being kind.
Yet why do the pigeons seem smarter than me?
Perhaps they're the sages of lost history.

Echoes of a Question

I asked the stars if they mind being bright,
But they giggled and winked, lighting up the night.
The moon joined the chorus with silver-toned glee,
While I stood there pondering who's weirder, us or they?

A tree whispered softly, 'Just let it all flow,'
But I'm stuck in my thoughts like a slow-moving crow.
What's the key to wisdom? Do I need more cheese?
Ah, well… here's a riddle; where's my car keys?

Beyond the Horizon of Understanding

I sailed on my questions, the sea made me laugh,
The waves were like teachers; I took quite a bath.
A dolphin popped up, with a grin and a splash,
'Just swim with the tide, don't worry, make a dash!'

The clouds shaped a castle, I waved to a dog,
Who barked back in echoes, 'Stop pulling that log!'
To find what I seek, it's a complicated mess,
Especially when socks are considered success.

Footsteps in the Dark

I tripped on a sock, it laughed at me,
My thoughts left a trail, like lost puppy.
I swore I could hear them, late in the night,
But all I found was my cat in the light.

I stumbled on secrets, a jar of jam,
That promised me wisdom, but tasted like spam.
With each step I took, I checked my shoe,
'Is finding the answer a game of peek-a-boo?'

Labyrinth of Awareness

I ventured through mazes of wisdom's embrace,
Where dead ends and mirrors just filled up the space.
I asked for directions, got lost in my thought,
Turns out that the answers were all for naught!

I chatted with gnomes, they were cheeky and bold,
Who offered me riddles much older than gold.
They'd chuckle and wink, then vanish with glee,
'Knowledge is great, but laughter's the key!'

Navigating the Ocean of Thought

I sailed on ideas, a boat made of dreams,
With waves of confusion and currents of memes.
The fish that I caught would just flip out and say,
'You want life's answers? Well, join the buffet!'

The sky opened wide, as I searched for some stars,
But they turned into frogs, chanting polka in cars.
Each splash in the water led me further astray,
'Perhaps I should fish for my socks, what a day!'

Searching for the Scattered Pieces

I gathered my thoughts like lost puzzle bits,
Each piece different shapes, and some even fit!
I flipped over cushions, I peeked under chairs,
Found a sock in the toaster and honest stares.

I asked my goldfish if he'd seen the way,
But he just swam circles, in bubbles at play.
I realized that searching can slip into fun,
When answers look silly, we've only begun!

The Journey of a Thousand Questions

Why does cheese always melt in the sun?
Is it truly a battle we've already won?
Can socks really disappear in the wash?
Or do they just party like little posh?

What's the deal with ducks quacking in sync?
Do they ponder life's meaning, or just like to wink?
Is pineapple pizza the answer we crave?
Or a joke from the taste buds that we can't save?

If clouds fluff up like a finished cake,
Do they hold secrets for us to take?
Must we follow the roads paved with gold?
Or just wander, while being bold?

Oh, the questions dance like a funny parade,
As we trip on the truths that we've often laid.
So we laugh, we search, we'll have some fun,
For every answer hides another one!

Light Through the Cracks

In the cupboard where old plates reside,
Is the best humor, where odd socks hide?
Can light sneak through every crevice and crack?
Do whispers of answers tumble right back?

Do cats conduct meetings at the break of dawn?
Are they plotting the way we keep yawning on?
When does an umbrella truly know rain?
Is it just for show, or to ease our pain?

If the stars fall just to tickle our dreams,
Are we the punchline of cosmic schemes?
Should we applaud, or just laugh at the jest?
The universe surely knows how to jest!

So let's embrace the quirks of it all,
With a chuckle that echoes, a comedic call.
Each problem leads to a pun we can share,
After all, who said we should always despair?

Explorations of the Beyond

What lies beyond the edge of the fridge?
Do spoons have feelings, or just take a bridge?
Can you hear the toaster's secrets unfold?
Or is it just another tale, all retold?

Is time a mere concept made up by clocks?
Or do they sneak gossip like tricky old fox?
When does a laugh turn into a snort?
When does fun leave and reason cavort?

Do fish ever wonder about life on land?
Or is their world just too perfectly planned?
Are we all just clues in this grand little game?
Or simply the punchlines, devoid of any fame?

So let's venture forth, map in our hand,
In search of the answers, both silly and grand.
With a wink and a grin, we'll keep rolling along,
For laughter's our compass, where we all belong!

Seeking the Heartbeat of Existence

I asked a frog for wisdom fair,
He croaked, then leapt without a care.
I gave a cat my finest treat,
It yawned and turned away its feet.

I roamed through fields of silly dreams,
Where cows breakdanced and penguins schemed.
The clouds, they chuckled, passing by,
And whispered secrets from the sky.

A squirrel tried to sell me hope,
With acorns packaged, promised cope.
I pondered hard, then burst in laughter,
For answers tease, yet lead to rafter.

In every jest, a truth takes flight,
In giggles loud, the dark turns bright.
I spin around with glee, I sigh,
Searching answers with a winked eye.

Lost in the Labyrinth

I entered a maze, or so I thought,
With twists and turns that life had wrought.
A signpost said, 'No exit here!'
A goose quacked loud, 'Just have some beer!'

I turned to find the way back home,
But ended up where hedgehogs roam.
They spun in circles, no sense at all,
I nearly tripped, but had a ball.

A minotaur grinned, said, 'What's the clue?'
I shrugged and said, 'Do you want stew?'
In jest we danced, lost in the wit,
Two foolish friends, in humor, we sit.

In hedges green, we cracked up loud,
Lost, yet found, in a silly crowd.
With every laugh, we lost the fear,
For wandering's fun when smiles are near.

Glimpses of Eternal Wonder

A star once winked, like a cheeky child,
It said to me, 'Life's nothing mild!'
I gazed in awe at its playful glow,
While clouds did pirouettes down below.

An owl screeched wisdom, quite bizarre,
'Life's a circus, be the star!'
I juggled thoughts like balls of light,
Until I dropped them, what a sight!

With every glance, the world would tease,
Like raindrops dancing on the breeze.
I laughed aloud at life's grand show,
Where questions bloom, yet answers flow.

So here I am, forever caught,
In giggles spun from every thought.
Chasing wonders, no end in sight,
Savoring moments, pure delight.

The Compass of Inquiry

I bought a compass made of cheese,
It spun around with perfect ease.
'This way!' it said, as I held tight,
Only to lead me to a kite.

The kite was laughing, in the sky,
I asked it, 'Why, oh why?' with a sigh.
It blankly stared then flew away,
Leaving me to figure the day.

A squirrel approached, with plans profound,
'Let's map a world where jokes abound!'
We drafted charts of silly schemes,
And sailed on boats of ice cream dreams.

With every step, absurdly clear,
Laughter filled the air, oh dear!
For truth is lost, yet here we roam,
In comedy's arms, we'll find our home.

Lanterns in the Abyss

In the dark, a lantern glows,
I ask it where the wisdom goes.
It flickers once, then makes a grin,
"If I knew, I'd surely win!"

I danced with shadows, eloped with air,
Asking clouds, they just don't care.
"Hey, Mr. Wind, what's life about?"
He laughs so hard, he blew me out!

The stars above join in the jest,
"There's no answer, forget the quest!"
So I twirl with joy in my slight despair,
And toast my woes with cosmic flair!

At dusk I ponder, half in jest,
Should I settle for less than the best?
But then a cricket hops near me,
Singing tunes of life's mystery!

Beyond the Veil of Reality

Beyond the veil, there's quite a scene,
Where questions swirl like ice cream.
I asked a ghost, with humor rife,
"What's the secret to a good life?"

He shrugged and sipped a phantom tea,
"Just don't take it all too seriously!"
A squirrel nearby snickered with glee,
"Life's best answer? Just let it be!"

I met a cat with three big eyes,
"Tell me, wise one, where wisdom lies?"
It purred and said, with a twitch of its tail,
"In every flop, there's a funny tale!"

I shrugged my shoulders and took a bow,
"Maybe answers aren't needed now.
Let's prance through nights with goofy delight,
For there's magic in every silly sight!"

The Canvas of Questions

Life's a canvas, paint it bold,
With brushstrokes bright and tales retold.
I asked my canvas, a splattered mess,
"Who's the king of this wild guess?"

It spat some paint as if to say,
"Grab your palette, let's paint the day!"
So I splashed and dashed with frolicsome haste,
Maybe life's best when not interlaced.

An owl perched, wise and true,
"You seeking answers? Just try the blue!"
I painted skies and fields of green,
Each stroke a quirky, wild scene!

So here's my take, oh painter friend,
Life's a giggle, not a trend.
With each brush, let laughter flow,
And cherish the whims of the colored show!

Searching for the Unseen

I went a-searching for sparkly things,
Like gold-plated wisdom or life's funny flings.
Met a frog who offered me a crown,
"Wear this, and you won't need a frown!"

Though the crown was just a twisty leaf,
I wore it proud and offered belief.
The frog then said, with a cheeky grin,
"Life's a joke, now hop on in!"

We leaped through bushes, giggled through trees,
Found wisdom wrapped in a gentle breeze.
"What's unseen?" I asked the night,
"It's laughter, friend, that's out of sight!"

So here we are, just hopping along,
With silly answers in a quirky song.
For when we're searching in playful strides,
The truth is hiding where humor abides!

Chronicles of the Unanswered

I asked the sky, where's the cheese?
It only chuckled, teasing with breeze.
The stars winked back in playful jest,
I just want answers, give it a rest!

The moon's a liar, says it's full
But it was half, now isn't that cruel?
I scribble questions that float like a kite,
Yet all I catch is the occasional bite!

The ocean roars, I dive for pearls,
Only to find—oh, just twirling swirls!
An octopus waves with a hat made of shells,
"What's the meaning?" I ask, he just yells!

In this quest, I wear silly shoes,
Stumbling and tripping, I can't pick and choose.
But laughter's the compass that guides me still,
With each laugh and giggle, I climb up the hill.

Beneath the Veil of Night

Under the stars, I tried to converse,
But they all sparkled, and I felt worse.
The moon did a dance, quite out of sight,
And giggled as I pondered, oh what a fright!

A comet zipped by, on a quest of its own,
"Find answers!" it shouted, then quickly was gone.
I waved my arms, in the dark of the sky,
But it only left me with questions awry.

The owls hooted in mysterious glee,
As I sat in the grass with my imaginary tea.
"Is life just a joke? A cosmic prank?"
My teacup emptied—ah, should have drank!

So here in the night, I embrace silly dreams,
Float through the darkness on laughter's sweet beams.
For though I seek meaning in shadows and light,
I find that the fun is in flying my kite!

The Dance of Questions and Dreams

In a ballroom where questions twirl and sway,
I asked a question—who stole my parfait?
The answers smirked in their dapper attire,
As I searched for sweets that I clearly desire!

The dreams crowded in, all dressed up in fluff,
"I need some wisdom!" I shouted, "That's enough!"
But they just giggled, did a little jig,
While I tried to solve this puzzling gig!

With a wink and a nod, the doubts took the floor,
"Who needs answers?" they whispered, "Let's dance some more!"
So I swung and I twirled in this frolicking spree,
In a world of silliness, happy as can be!

Perhaps the truth is just laughter in disguise,
Winking at me from those sparkling skies.
So let's twinkle and jiggle, and dance with delight,
For the pursuit of knowledge sure feels pretty bright!

In Pursuit of the Elusive Light

Chasing the sun on a rubbery boat,
I hollered aloud, but it wouldn't gloat.
"Where's the wisdom?" I called to the waves,
They splashed back loudly, just mischief and braves!

In the forest of puzzles, I wandered all day,
Chasing my tail and lost on the way.
A squirrel rolled by on a unicycle seat,
"Life's just a game; enjoy the sweet treat!"

The fireflies twinkled, leading the chase,
But I stumbled over roots, fell flat on my face.
"Hey, who left this here?" I frowned at the ground,
The light just winked back; it seemed so profound!

So here I am, chasing the whimsical glow,
With giggles and chuckles as I come and go.
For the search for answers is wrapped up in glee,
In this fun little journey, it's just you and me!

Whispers in the Void

In the dark, I hear a sound,
A sock that's lost, it spins around.
It whispers tales of places unknown,
Of missing keys and seeds I've sown.

The fridge hums softly, a friendly ghost,
It tells me where I've left my toast.
While shadows dance and giggle with glee,
They hide the answers, just like me.

Paths of the Wanderer

With breadcrumbs dropped from hasty feet,
I wander roads where lost socks meet.
A map unfolds with doodles drawn,
Leading me to where the laughter's born.

I ask a bird, 'What's the secret?'
It chirps a tune, then flies off, sweet.
The ducks just quack, and waddle away,
Leaving me to ponder, come what may.

Glimpses of the Hidden

Behind the couch, I find a shoe,
It once was lost, now smells like stew.
With every peek, I face delight,
Where pretzels hide and dust bunnies bite.

A mirror shows me silly faces,
While I chase thoughts in hidden places.
It whispers gently, 'Don't take a stroll,
Today you'll find your missing soul!'

The Stillness of Questions

In the quiet, questions bloom,
Like flowers growing in the gloom.
What's the meaning behind a sneeze?
Or why do cats think they own the bees?

The moon just smiles with a knowing wink,
As I sit and ponder while I think.
The answers might be lost, it's true,
But hey, at least I found my shoe!

Journeys Beyond Understanding

I packed my bags with hopes and dreams,
Setting off on wild, silly schemes.
I asked a frog for some profound signs,
He just croaked back, 'Life's full of lines.'

I wandered far through hills and streams,
Chasing after those glittery beams.
Found a wise old turtle who just sighed,
Said, 'Kid, it's all just a fun ride!'

With every map I drew askew,
I realized my compass was a shoe.
I danced with shadows, laughed with trees,
Life's prickly thoughts blown by the breeze.

A search for meaning in every jest,
Frolicking through life's confusing quest.
So here I am, embracing the gaff,
Searching for answers while sharing a laugh.

The Horizon of Dreams

I sailed my ship on a sea of whim,
Hoping to find the edge of a dream.
The clouds just giggled, the stars gave a wink,
And I swore the moon just wanted to drink.

With a map drawn in crayon, I charted my way,
Bumping into mermaids asking me to stay.
But when I said 'no,' they cackled in fun,
'Life's too short, better ride on the sun!'

I found a whale who dubbed me 'brave,'
He offered me fish for a funny rave.
We laughed until dawn, both quite absurd,
Searching for answers that never occurred.

Oh, the treasure is in the silly turns,
In dance-party waves where laughter burns.
So here I float on this wave of a tune,
Chasing horizons and a cheeky balloon.

Reflections on the Sea of Being

I peered into the water, a mirror so bright,
Saw a fish in a tuxedo, what a sight!
He winked and said, 'Life's quite a show,'
'Just follow the bubbles; they surely know.'

I dove for meaning, but found only sand,
With a crab who recited Shakespeare on command.
He said, 'To be, my friend, is quite a jest,
Just pinch your worries and don't stop to rest.'

I floated on thoughts like driftwood on tides,
Sharing my musings with jellyfish guides.
They floated beneath, all giddy and bright,
Lending me wisdom wrapped in the night.

With laughter echoing through depths of my mind,
I learned that the journey's the best kind.
So heed not the answers; just follow your cheer,
For life's funny puzzles are meant to endear.

The Searchlight of Insights

I took a stroll with a light in my hand,
Searching for answers—I made quite a band.
But the thoughts danced away, like fireflies at dusk,
Fleeing with giggles, like laughter, a must.

With each little spark, I tried to compose,
A symphony of knowledge, or so I supposed.
But the gears in my head played a jumbled song,
They tripped on the beat, oh, it all felt so wrong!

Along came a squirrel who tried to share,
Insights so grand, he'd a nut for a pair.
'You seek the truth? Just look for the nuts!
Life's too short to be tangled with ruts!'

And as I pondered, the searchlight grew dim,
Revealing the joy—not the work within.
So I let the light dance, I laughed and let go,
For maybe the answers are not the main show.

Fragments of Light

In a jar, I keep my dreams,
Hoping they don't burst at the seams.
A shoelace here, a sock there,
Searching hard, but life seems rare.

A frog in the fridge, what's it for?
Perhaps to remind me, just explore.
If lemons give me zest, oh so bright,
Should I squeeze them with all my might?

Ideas float like balloons in the air,
Sometimes they pop, sometimes they scare.
With laughter I chase what could be fun,
Even if it's just a runaway bun.

I'll wear mismatched shoes, just for a start,
To show the cosmos my creative heart.
With each silly twist and nonsensical turn,
I find snippets of wisdom that I yearn.

Reflections in a Cosmic Mirror

I looked into a starry glass,
And saw my reflection in a little green gas.
Am I an alien or just misplaced?
Wondering if jellybeans are really my taste?

Cosmic ducks quack in endless rows,
While I'm here questioning my hair's woes.
Is UFO in my kitchen? Oh, what a sight!
What's next, a dance with a pirate at night?

Mirror, mirror, are you real or jest?
Do you hold the secrets or just a big pest?
I tried to find answers in a piece of toast,
But it just burned, what a cosmic roast!

Life's a circus, seats all around,
And I'm the clown with shoes unbound.
With a wink and a jest, I sashay with glee,
For every giggle shares a clue with me.

Journeys Through the Unknown

I packed my bags with snacks and cheer,
Off to lands where no one fears.
Maybe a dragon will serve me tea,
Or a wise old sage with a bad knee.

I rode a whale, we danced with the moon,
But he slipped on a banana, oh what a tune!
Exploring places far and wide,
Stumbling over every cosmic slide.

Was that a talking cactus in the sand?
With hats made of silver, the finest in the land.
I asked for directions, he just sighed,
Then offered me jelly, which I gladly tried.

Each step I take, a giggle escapes,
As I meet odd creatures in curious shapes.
Through laughs and blunders, I find my way,
In this cosmic puzzle, let's dance and play.

The Dance of Possibilities

With a fanciful twirl and a skip, I pranced,
Inviting quirky dreams to join in the dance.
Come meet the unicorns with shades of pink,
We'll giggle and glow while we think and rethink.

A walrus in a bow tie showed me the beat,
While jellybeans rapped with quick little feet.
Possibilities flutter like butterflies bright,
Each wave of laughter adds sparks to the night.

The chicken waltzed past, clucking in style,
While I tossed confetti with a silly smile.
In the cha-cha of quirks, we spin and sway,
Life's odd little rhythms lead us astray.

Shy wishes peek out like stars from the sky,
Why not let the weird ones dance on by?
In the carnival of errors, we'll find our flair,
For every misstep, there's magic to share.

Poets of the Unknown

In the realm of cosmic jest,
Winking stars always know best.
They giggle at our silly plight,
Chasing clues in the dead of night.

With magnifying glasses in hand,
We search for answers on the sand.
Finding crabs with a twist of fate,
Laughing loud at our own debate.

A wise old turtle glanced our way,
"Stop searching, mate! Let's dance and sway!"
He taught us to leap with delight,
As the Moon played tunes with sheer delight.

So, we frolic 'neath cosmic lights,
Trading questions for silly flights.
Inquirers with a twist of fate,
Finding answers a little late.

Chronicles of an Endless Journey

On this wild ride, we start to roam,
With packed bags and a squeaky gnome.
Every corner brings a new surprise,
Like socks that vanish without goodbyes.

We ask the trees where dreams take flight,
They whisper back, "Try the left at night!"
Guided by birds with hats so bright,
Who knew wisdom could be such a sight?

With maps drawn in crayon, what a mess!
Yet every wrong turn leads to success.
A garden of laughter, jokes on the way,
Every stumble is worth the play!

So we tumble through this curious maze,
With lost keys and confusing days.
In the chronicles of humorous sights,
We chase answers while flying kites.

Songs of the Unexplored

Beneath the couch, oh what a find!
A sock, a toy, and peace of mind.
We sing for joy, let's belt it out,
In this kingdom, there's nary a doubt!

With a spoon as a microphone in hand,
We croon to the walls of our homey land.
Every echo brings laughter wide,
As dust bunnies join our joyful ride.

In the garage, treasures wait in stacks,
Like old bikes telling tales with cracks.
We dance among the wreckage bold,
Singing sweet tunes till we're old.

So, let's make tunes from life's oddball zest,
Discovering joy in every quest.
In the songs of the unexplored here,
We find our answers wrapped in cheer!

In the Wilderness of Thought

In the jungle of musings, we roam so free,
Chasing wild questions like a buzzing bee.
With ideas that dance on the edge of sanity,
We ponder if cats plot a whole vanity.

With pencils as swords, we duel with our minds,
Wrestling with thoughts, each twist and grind.
The trees roll their eyes, they've seen it all,
While squirrels debate with a chuckle and sprawl.

There's wisdom in chaos, or so they say,
As we tumble through thoughts that lead us astray.
A riddle awaits in the heart of a dream,
Where nothing is truly as simple as it seems.

So, embark on this wild, whimsical chase,
Finding answers in the silliest place.
In the wilderness of thought, we discover,
Life's a riddle, let's all be a lover!

Riddles Weaving Through Time

Why did the clock take a break?
It wanted to know, what's at stake?
Tick-tock, it pondered in glee,
Time's just a joke, or so it seems to me.

What if a leaf could really talk?
It'd shout about its stroll on the block.
'Hey squirrel, quit stealing my show!'
Life's just a giggle if you go with the flow.

The cat asked the dog, 'What's your quest?'
The dog just barked, 'To find the best!'
But who knew that chasing tails is the score,
In this silly game of we want more?

So let's toast to the queries we raise,
With laughter and chuckles, we'll fill our days.
Ask away, with popcorn in hand,
For life's quirks are the finest in this land.

Exploring the Uncharted

Why did the map feel so lost?
It couldn't find its way, at any cost.
'North, south, east, or could it be west?'
Even directions can take a rest!

The compass spins, a dizzy old friend,
'Am I lost again? How does this end?'
With humor, it points all over the place,
Searching for something in empty space.

Aliens called, from galaxies afar,
'What's this Earth game? Is it bizarre?'
They laughed at our selfies, our 'wish you were here'
Injecting us with cosmic good cheer.

So let's sail the seas of "what if" and "why,"
On ships made of laughter, we'll let our minds fly.
With each uncharted giggle we find,
The treasure's the fun that we leave behind.

The Enigma of Existence

What's the secret of a potato chip?
It's a crunchy riddle, take a dip.
Salty thoughts, ever up for a munch,
Life's answers are best served with lunch.

A cat walks in, wearing a tie,
Says, 'I'm here for the philosophical pie.'
With a whisker twitch and a knowing stare,
'To exist is to snack, if you dare!'

A goldfish pondered inside its bowl,
'Is swimming in circles the meaning of soul?'
With a flip of its fin, it swam with a grin,
Finding essence in bubbles and spin.

So spare us your wisdom, dear sphinx on the shelf,
For we're just here to laugh at ourselves.
Existence might baffle, but take a seat,
With humor, we'll dance, and life's bittersweet.

Clues in Cosmic Silence

The universe whispered a clue in the night,
A giggle of stardust, all shining bright.
'What's it all for? Ha-ha! No stress!'
Sometimes the silence tells us the best.

A comet zoomed by, with a wink and a grin,
'Who can guess how long this ride has been?'
With laughter in orbit, they spun round a star,
Maybe the answer's just how funny we are.

A moonbeam chuckled, 'Hey sun, take a break!'
'You shine too hard, for goodness' sake!'
With warmth in the cosmos, they shared a dance,
Life's a whimsical waltz, if you give it a chance.

So here's to the clues we find through the jest,
In the silence of cosmos, we can find rest.
For laughter ignites a spark in the dark,
And the quest for the answers? Just a cosmic lark!

Harmonies of Search and Yearning

I asked a turtle, wise and old,
"Where can I find treasures untold?"
He just shrugged and munched on a leaf,
Said, "Buddy, you're chasing your belief!"

A squirrel chimed in from a nearby tree,
"The answer's in snacks, not philosophy!"
I pondered this while munching some nuts,
Life's riddle might just be in our guts!

The ants paraded, all lined in a row,
They whispered secrets, soft and low.
"We're all busy in our little sway,
But no one has figured it out, hey?"

So I laughed with the bugs, what a hoot!
The quest for truth felt quite like a flute.
Each note a giggle, a joyous refrain,
Guess we're all searching—just in our own lane!

A Symphony of Wonder

A chicken clucked on the farm today,
"What's the point?" I heard her say.
"We lay eggs in the sun, so bright,
But why on earth, are we in this plight?"

A pig rolled by, covered in muck,
He snorted, "Maybe it's just bad luck!"
"What do we eat at the end of our spree?
Tacos or hay? Oh, woe is me!"

The ducks quacked loud with a splash in the pond,
"Sing 'la la la' and just bob along!"
In harmony, we danced around,
Life's goofy answers, nowhere to be found!

So we waddle, and cluck, and wallow in glee,
Chasing our tails, as dumb as can be.
With joy in our hearts and food on the way,
Maybe laughter's the answer to every hooray!

Beneath the layers of Knowing

A wise old owl perched high up a tree,
Grinned down at me, said, "Just be free!"
"What's underneath all this fluff and strife?
It's probably just another cat's life!"

I scrunched my face, puzzled and vexed,
"Is life just a game, what are the specs?"
A rabbit hopped in, ears flopping around,
"Dude, hop along! Don't just stand on the ground!"

We gathered a crowd, the crickets and bees,
Held a debate on how to sneeze.
"Achoo!" said one—"See? That's profound!
Maybe the answer's where laughter is found!"

So beneath all the drama and layers we see,
What matters most is just being silly.
For in giggles and snickers, we find our delight,
And navigate life with a smile, not fright!

Threads of Life's Tapestry

In a fabric shop of dreams and of seams,
Threaded with laughter and wild, quirky themes.
A seamstress said, with a thread in her hand,
"The secret to life is just to expand!"

Stitch upon stitch, reality's sewn,
In colors so bright, we've merrily grown.
"See that yarn ball?" chimed a voice from below,
"It's just tangled thoughts that put on a show!"

So we wove our fears into something so grand,
Laughter the needle, creativity the strand.
"Embrace your oddities, let them unwind,
In this quilt of existence, we'll all be aligned!"

With each little poke and a merry little twist,
We unravel and laugh at the things we have missed.
These threads we call life are wild and absurd,
But stitch by stitch, we find joy in the word!

The Breath of Silent Thoughts

In a quiet room, I ponder deep,
Why does my cat always leap?
With whiskers twitching and eyes aglow,
Perhaps she knows what I don't know.

Chasing shadows, she prances about,
I'm left here wondering, with a pout.
Answers hide where the fish may swim,
Yet she just stares as I sink, not swim.

With laundry tumbling, my mind goes gray,
Searching for wisdom that's on holiday.
Maybe the sock's advice can help,
Or is it just nonsense of the lonesome kelp?

With tea in hand, I raise a toast,
To all the questions I fear the most.
So here's to laughter and curious glee,
Maybe the truth's just hiding with me.

Unraveling Tapestries of Wonder

I knit with yarn of cosmic thread,
Hoping for wisdom instead of dread.
My needles clack like clockwork mice,
Yet all I get is a tangled slice.

Patterns emerge, then fray in haste,
A scarf of doubts wrapped 'round my waist.
I try to weave a tapestry bright,
But end up frowning, as stitches fight.

The cat pounces, oh what a scene,
Here, all the threads are not what they seem.
So I ask the universe for a clue,
And it responds with a sneeze and a chew.

Laughter echoes in the loom of fate,
As I realize I'm not the one to create.
Life's knitted wonders will come when they're right,
And until then, I'll enjoy the delight.

Wandering in the Forest of Doubt

Lost in the woods where the squirrels play,
I'm trying to find my lost way.
The trees are tall, their secrets steep,
But all they do is whisper and sleep.

A rabbit winks, but won't share the book,
Of answers hidden in nooks or crannies—what a rook!
I trip on roots, curse the day,
Where's the MapQuest for my disarray?

Birds sing sweetly, but sing of which cheese?
Their tunes just flutter on the breeze.
"Follow the breadcrumbs," I scold with a grin,
But then I discover I'm lost once more within.

With a chuckle, I dance through the sprigs,
Where questions spin like hula hoops and jigs.
Maybe it's fun to lose my route,
In this forest of doubt, I'll laugh, there's no doubt!

The Fruitless Quest for Clarity

My quest for clarity begins with a wink,
Armed with a pen and an empty drink.
I scribble notes with the grace of a seal,
While elusive answers scamper, like eels.

Pages spread wide like butterflies' wings,
But wisdom hops off, doing silly things.
It tickles my brain, and I start to cry,
My doodles grow legs and skip by.

A wise old turtle interrupts my plight,
"Slow down, my friend, it's all quite alright."
He scoffs at my papers, strewn all about,
Says clarity's nonsense, and that's the route.

So I laugh with the turtle, we dance in the sun,
No need for answers, just join in the fun.
For life's quite the riddle, clever and spry,
With questions afloat like popcorn in the sky.

Interstellar Searches

In a rocket shaped like a fish,
I zoom past stars on my wild wish.
Do aliens know how to dance?
Or just sit and watch, in a trance?

With a telescope made from soda cans,
I try to decipher their silly plans.
Maybe they're hiding under the moon,
Watching Earth's folks in a wild cartoon.

I tried to contact Mars with a joke,
But I think their humor's gone up in smoke.
What do you get when you cross a star?
A bright little thing driving a space car!

So I tickle the cosmic phone and say,
"Hey, extraterrestrials, wanna play?"
But all I hear is a chipmunk's song,
Guess they're busy; I'll just hum along!

Fables of Existence

Once in a world of marshmallow trees,
Lived a philosopher who couldn't sneeze.
He pondered life while eating pie,
"Why do we exist?" he asked the sky.

The stars twinkled back with a giggle,
"Maybe you need to do a little jiggle!"
So he wiggled and jiggled, made quite a scene,
And found his answer in a jellybean.

The creatures of thought, dressed in boots,
Told tales of travels and cosmic scoots.
They said, "Life's a fable, like socks with holes,
A wild ride filled with lost toes!"

I laughed so hard, I almost cried,
Life's mysteries are best enjoyed wide.
So kick up your feet, grab that starfish,
For answers are found in a twist of the wrist!

In Pursuit of Essence

A chicken crossed the cosmic street,
To find the answers it thought were neat.
"Why did you cross?" asked a wise old toad,
"Just hunting for meaning on this bumpy road."

The chicken clucked and hopped around,
Searching in the air, under grass, and ground.
"Is it in the worm?" it wondered aloud,
"Or maybe the clouds, all fluffy and proud?"

Then a cow floated by, wearing a cape,
"I've found the truth, and it's quite a shape!"
The chicken asked, "What's it like?"
"A circle, of course! Now, life's a bike!"

So they rode together to the edge of space,
Finding laughter and puzzlement in every place.
With each goofy turn, they gleefully confessed,
The answer is fun, and that's simply the best!

Stories Written in Starlight

Under the glow of a moonlit tale,
A space cat spun yarns like a fuzzy trail.
"Did you hear about the snail who flew?
He whispered to stars, 'Hey, look at me too!'"

In coffee cups, planets peeped and pried,
Tap dancing on comets with laughter and pride.
They wrote poems with rings from Jupiter's bling,
Finding wisdom in jokes that we all love to sing.

A spaceship made of candy canes zoomed by,
With astronauts who would sip lemonade sky-high.
"Down on Earth, they think they know,"
"But we've found the secrets in the sprinkles' glow!"

So gather round, and let's share delight,
In stories spun bright with starlight.
For life's quirks and quips, oh what a ride,
Adventures await on the cosmic tide!

Endless Echoes of Existence

In a quest for the answers bright,
I tripped over the cat last night.
She eyed me with great disdain,
As if I held the world's last grain.

My coffee spilled, a potent brew,
Swirled clues I never really knew.
The spoon sighed, the mug gave a frown,
Why's wisdom always upside down?

Questions bounce, like a rubber ball,
Ricochet thoughts, then they stall.
I asked a tree, it just shrugged,
Leaves gossiping, feeling snug.

As I ponder, my socks don't match,
Life's riddle like an awkward patch.
Perhaps the answer's in this mess,
Or did I just forget the dress?

Whispered Queries of the Soul

Amidst the stars, I raised a brow,
Expecting answers, and a cow!
The moon winked and fell off its chair,
While gravity laughed without a care.

I asked a fish, it swam away,
Was that a yes, or just cliché?
Seagulls giggled from high above,
Plotting their next move, not love.

A snail gave me wisdom slow,
"Fast isn't always the way to go."
I blinked twice, then slowly agreed,
Life's more about the fun, indeed!

So I twirled and danced in the sun,
Chasing shadows, oh what fun!
If answers lurk in giggles and glee,
Who knew searching could be so free?

Navigating the Labyrinth of Thought

In the maze of thoughts, I roam,
Chasing riddles, far from home.
A signpost pointed left, or was it right?
The squirrel watched my silly plight.

With maps all drawn in crayon hue,
I sought wisdom from a shoe.
It said, "Just walk, you might be late,"
But wisdom's timing is first-rate.

Around each corner, questions sprout,
Like weeds popping up, all about.
I asked a mirror, it cracked a smile,
"Who's the fairest? Walk that aisle!"

Amidst the chaos, laughs abound,
In every turn, joys are found.
Life's riddles wrapped in giggles bright,
Keep wandering 'til you find the light.

Beyond the Horizon of Understanding

I set my sights on distant dreams,
With a sandwich pack filled with schemes.
A compass spun in a funky dance,
While I pondered life's great chance.

The clouds above just drifted by,
Painting answers in the sky.
They whispered softly, "Take a break!"
But I was busy, for goodness' sake!

In the distance, a laughing fool,
Danced in circles, skipped the school.
He shouted, "Life's a big buffet!"
I fell for it, and lost my way.

Yet every misstep gives a grin,
A treasure found where doubts have been.
So let's explore this comedy spree,
For the answers hide in joviality!

Illuminating the Shadows of Hope

In a world of lost socks, we seek the truth,
Mismatched queries dance, revel in our youth.
Chasing down answers like cats chase the light,
We laugh at the shadows that loom in the night.

With a spoonful of humor and a big jar of dreams,
We trip over questions like odd, tangled seams.
Caught in a riddle that jigs like a tune,
We giggle and ponder 'neath the watchful moon.

Questions are sprinkles on life's cupcake treat,
Who knew contemplation could be so sweet?
Finding out answers, oh what a fun game,
Especially when the butt of the joke is the same!

So raise up your glasses, let's toast to the quest,
For the joy in the journey, we count as a jest.
In the land of the silly, where giggles abound,
We'll keep on exploring, for wisdom is found!

The Song of Endless Inquiry

Why do we wonder? Oh, it's just our style,
Asking odd questions while grinning all the while.
Is vanilla really a flavor of snow?
Or am I just hungry? I'd like to know!

Like treasure maps scribbled on napkins and dreams,
We ponder the universe, poking its seams.
Is silence really golden, or just plain dull?
Let's throw in some giggles, it makes life full!

With each silly riddle that tickles the mind,
We find that the journey's the best, I'm inclined.
As we sing silly songs of our wild, crazy plight,
We embrace every question with sheer delight.

So let's dance through the chaos, where laughter ignites,
Around all the mysteries that shine through the nights.
In this grand ol' inquiry, with hearts that are bold,
We'll find that the punchline's the joy to behold!

Eternal Queries

What makes the stars twinkle, a cosmic charade?
Is it just an illusion, a brilliant facade?
Why do onions make us cry, is it their flair?
Or do they just want us to show that we care?

Chasing these questions, like squirrels on a spree,
Why wear matching socks? Be as wild as can be!
Life's just a puzzle, with pieces askew,
Yet each silly search has a humor or two.

Let's tickle the brain with a quest for the weird,
Jumping through hoops, oh, how we've cheered!
From ducks that quack answers to goats that can sing,
Logic takes a backseat as we laugh at the swing.

So here's to our queries, both quirky and bright,
They tumble like raindrops, a most splendid sight.
In the dance of confusion where chaos can thrive,
We find through the laughter, the joy to survive!

Whispers of the Cosmos

The cosmos whispers, 'Hey, what's your deal?'
Each question a giggle, a cosmic ideal.
Why do we joke about interstellar flight?
When we surely can't navigate at night!

Shooting for answers like marbles in space,
We tumble through mysteries, all in good grace.
Do penguins wear tuxes when they go out to play?
If life is a party, who's DJing today?

In a galaxy funky, with stars in their socks,
We ponder the meaning of paradox clocks.
Round and around, for the joy of the game,
We find in the laughter, we're all quite the same.

So raise your binoculars, peer into the skies,
Let's chase down the riddles with sparkle in our eyes.
As we whisper with stars and tickle the air,
The answers are funny, if we only dare!

Wings of Contemplation

A chicken crossed the road, so bold,
To ponder truths yet to be told.
With wings flapping wide in search of a clue,
Squawking loudly, "Is that life in the view?"

Butterflies flutter, but don't know the score,
While ants in a line just march out the door.
Seeking wisdom from flowers in bloom,
They whisper, "What's tasty? Can we dodge the doom?"

A cat named Whiskers thinks deep thoughts at night,
As he chases shadows and dodges the light.
He wonders aloud with a twitch of his tail,
"Is tuna an answer? Or am I just frail?"

The clouds roll in, with visions to share,
Each one a question floating in air.
Giraffes munch leaves, while thinking about,
"Could life be simpler, without any doubt?"

Stars Aligned with Curiosity

Under the moon, a wise old owl,
Ponders the universe with a hoot and a howl.
He asks the stars, with a flick of his wing,
"Are we just here for this song we sing?"

A comet zooms by, with a zippy long tail,
Yelling, "Life's a journey, set sail, set sail!"
Planets all laugh, twirling round in the dark,
"We're just spinning dust, let's make more spark!"

Rabbits debate under starlit delight,
"Is life just a game or an endless flight?"
They play hopscotch with stars, as they munch on grass,
In a galaxy filled with pop and some sass.

Martians watch over, with their big buggy eyes,
Wondering if Earthlings ever tell lies.
"Do they even know they're just playing a part?"
While sipping stardust, they chart out the heart.

Echoes of the Unanswered

In a coffee shop, deep thoughts brew,
Baristas serve answers with a side of 'who knew?'
With frothy tops, they ponder aloud,
"If beans hold wisdom, are we allowed?"

A squirrel takes notes, nibbling on cake,
"What's life's big question? I'm wide awake!"
He scribbles furiously on a napkin torn,
"Is it bad if I say I'm just slightly worn?"

Fish in a bowl debate with their gills,
"Is swimming in circles really giving us thrills?"
They bubble and burst, trying hard to concur,
"Let's get out of here; do we even prefer?"

The echoes of laughter bounce off the walls,
Truths wrapped in humor, like jokes in the halls.
Life's silly riddles, all tangled and bright,
Remind us to chuckle while we search for light.

Parables of Perception

A wise old tortoise, slow as can be,
Reflects on existence while sipping his tea.
"Is speed just an illusion in this fast-paced race?"
He smiles to himself, finding joy in each space.

Parrots squawk loudly, mimicking what's said,
"Is it truth if all we parrot's in our head?"
With feathers all ruffled, they laugh and they preen,
Feeling quite clever, although rather green.

Through woods, mischievous rabbits hop around,
Chasing their shadows, what wisdom they've found!
"Do we need answers when the grass is so sweet?"
They munch on their greens, enjoying the beat.

In a world full of quirks, dear friends, let's embrace,
The funny follies in life's endless chase.
For wrapped in the jest, we might just discover,
That each little moment could lead us to wonder.

Unwritten Pages of Existence

Why do socks always disappear?
Are they off to a party in the stratosphere?
Pants go missing, left high and dry,
Are they just dreaming of a sky-high fly?

In the fridge, that carrot's growing old,
It dreams of glory, or so I'm told.
Peas all piled in a messy pile,
Whispering secrets and having a trial.

The dog wags tails, thinking they rule,
While cats sit there, acting like fools.
Chasing the shadows, the sun and the grass,
What do they know? They're just living fast!

Life's a puzzle, but hey, it's a game,
You might find a cat, but not the same.
Hold on to laughter, let it fly high,
For answers are buried in a wink and a sigh.

Unveiling the Cosmic Puzzle

Aliens texting from afar,
Asking for tips on how to bake a pie.
Stars are giggling, the planets all dance,
What if they're just after a good romance?

Gravity's always pulling us down,
Except when we trip, then we rally around.
Jumping and falling, it's quite a sight,
Perhaps life's riddle is simply a fright.

Jellybeans plotting in candy-coated nights,
Debating if jelly is what gives them flights.
Glitches in time in a cosmic board game,
But who really knows who's the one to blame?

We're but stardust with socks mismatched,
Doing our best, but often detached.
So wave to the universe, give it a cheer,
The puzzle is funny when you're filled with beer!

Imprints on the Sands of Time

Footprints leading to the ice cream stand,
A trail of sprinkles left in the sand.
Where do they go? To flavors unknown,
Maybe to space on a pink taffy throne?

Waves crash, washing dreams all away,
Leaving behind a message to play.
Seashells giggle, trapped in a drift,
Hoping to hear the tide's next gift.

Time ticks away like a busted clock,
Each tick can spark a new funny shock.
A sandwich lost in a cosmic swirl,
Maybe it's out having a grand twirl!

Each moment a waltz on the beach of the now,
A dance with the future, don't ask me how.
Share a laugh with those grains of sand,
For life's little quirks are simply unplanned.

Mysteries Beneath the Surface

What lurks in the depths of the deep, dark sea?
A fish in pajamas? A turtle with glee?
Corals gossip about the fish they adore,
While seaweed just dances, begging for more.

Octopuses scribble notes on the floor,
Arguing over who's the best dancer on tour.
Is that a whale with a tune in its throat?
Or just a bubble from a sleepy old goat?

The crabs orchestrate an undersea show,
Snap their pincers to say, 'Look at me go!'
Jellyfish float with dreams of a sun,
But all they've got is a glimmering fun.

Beneath the surface lay secrets galore,
Whispers of laughter wash up on the shore.
Dive in, take a plunge, don't think twice,
For even in depths, there's always a slice!

www.ingramcontent.com/pod-product-compliance
Lightning Source LLC
Chambersburg PA
CBHW071822160426
43209CB00003B/172